Life on the
ORINOCO

Rob Waring, *Series Editor*

HEINLE
CENGAGE Learning

Australia • Brazil • Japan • Korea • Mexico • Singapore • Spain • United Kingdom • United States

Words to Know

This story is set in South America. It starts near Brazil and goes through the country of Venezuela. It happens on the Orinoco [ɔrɪnoᵤkoᵤ] River.

 Landscapes of the Orinoco. Read the definitions and look at the picture below. Write the number of the correct underlined word next to each item.

1. The ocean is a very large body of water; a sea.
2. A delta is the place where a big river enters the sea.
3. Mountains are very high areas of land.
4. A large area of flat land is called a plain.
5. A waterfall is a place where water is falling from a higher area.
6. A river is a large body of water that moves in one direction.
7. A stream is a small body of water that moves in one direction.
8. A rain forest is a large area of trees and other plants where it rains every day.

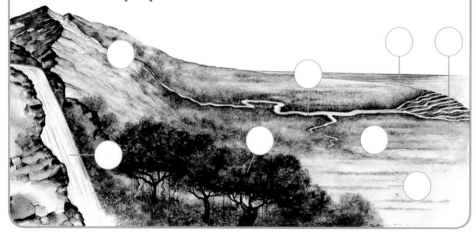

B **Animals of the Orinoco.** Here are some wild animals you will find in the story. Label the picture with the words in the box.

anaconda
capybara [kæpɪbeɪrə]
crocodile
jaguar
piranha [pɪrɑnyə]

1. _____

4. _____

2. _____

3. _____

5. _____

The Orinoco River in South America is one of the longest rivers in the world. It starts in the mountains of Venezuela and Brazil. It then **flows**[1] for nearly **1,300 miles**[2] to its delta on the Atlantic Ocean.

On its way south, the Orinoco flows through many different landscapes. It moves past **ancient**[3] stone formations, over waterfalls, through rain forest areas, and across large plains.

---

[1]**flow:** move forward; usually continuously and easily
[2]**1,300 miles:** 2,092 kilometers
[3]**ancient:** very old

🎧 CD 1, Track 09

The Orinoco Delta is the area where the river's water flows into the ocean. The area around the delta is full of streams and small waterways. These smaller rivers, or tributaries, connect to the larger Orinoco. One of these tributaries, called the **Caroni**,[4] features Angel Falls. Angel Falls is the highest waterfall in the world!

---

[4] **Caroni:** [kɑrəni]

Angel Falls, which is on an Orinoco tributary, is the highest waterfall in the world.

However, there's more than just water in the delta. The Orinoco Delta is also home to several South American Indian cultures. They have lived next to the river for thousands of years and they still live there today. Actually, the name 'Orinoco' comes from a local language. It means 'place to **paddle**'.[5]

One of these Orinoco Indian cultures is the **Yanomami**.[6] About two thousand Yanomami people live near the river, far from the rest of the world. For them, and about twenty other local cultures, the Orinoco is an important **natural resource**.[7] The river not only gives them a means of travel, but also a supply of clean water and food. The Orinoco River greatly supports these traditional cultures.

---

[5] **paddle:** move a small boat through water with a short piece of flat wood

[6] **Yanomami:** [yænəmɑmi]

[7] **natural resource:** things which naturally exist in a place and can be used by people

a waterway

a paddle

The rain forest around the Orinoco River has many kinds of plants and animals. It is home to more than a thousand different types of birds. In the river itself, there are many types of fish—including the dangerous piranha! And on the land around the river, you'll find even more interesting animals. . .

… like the Orinoco crocodile. He may have a big smile, but be careful! These animals can grow to more than **18 feet**[8] long! This makes the Orinoco crocodile one of the longest crocodiles in the world.

There are big snakes on the Orinoco River too. One of the biggest is the anaconda. It's one of the largest kinds of snakes in the world.

In the rain forest, you may have a chance to see one of the area's beautiful jaguars. But on the open plains, you will more likely see a totally different animal—the world's biggest **rodent**,[9] the capybara.

---

[8]**18 feet:** 6.10 meters
[9]**rodent:** a kind of small animal with long, sharp teeth

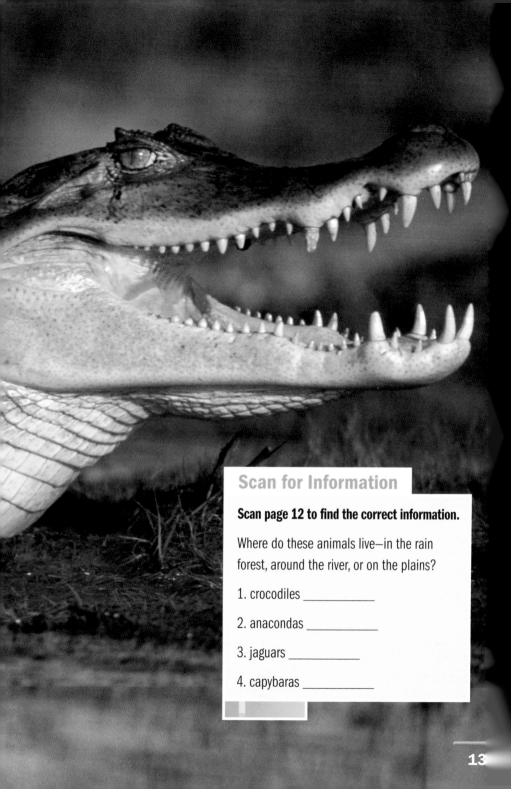

Scan for Information

Scan page 12 to find the correct information.

Where do these animals live—in the rain forest, around the river, or on the plains?

1. crocodiles _____

2. anacondas _____

3. jaguars _____

4. capybaras _____

However, over the past fifty years, things have changed along the Orinoco River. Some of the cities and towns have grown significantly. These cities have also taken some of the land where animals and plants once were. The new industrial world is slowly coming to the Orinoco Delta. But what industries have been introduced? More importantly, what are they doing to the beautiful river, its animals, and its people?

Identify the Main Idea

1. What is the main idea of the paragraph on page 15?

2. What are two pieces of information that support this idea?

One of the industries that has grown is electricity production. Parts of the Orinoco now have **dams**[10] to help control the water. These dams also collect the river's water to create electrical power.

There are also other industries in the area as well. Companies there have found valuable products, like **gold**,[11] **diamonds**,[12] and **oil**.[13] Very big ships now travel up and down the river from the Atlantic Ocean to move these products.

---

[10] **dam:** a strong wall built across a river to stop the water
[11] **gold:** a valuable, shiny, yellow metal
[12] **diamonds:** very valuable clear stones
[13] **oil:** a thick black liquid that comes from under the ground

a dam

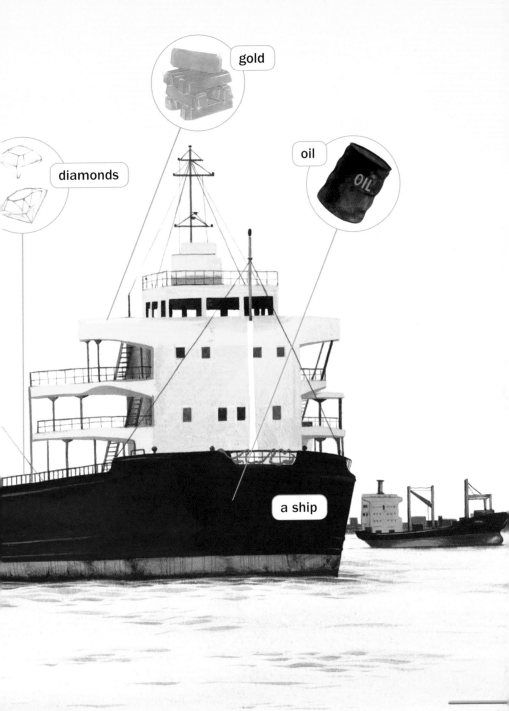

gold

diamonds

oil

a ship

It's clear that there have been some big changes on the Orinoco in recent years. But not everything has changed. Many sections of the river and the areas around them have stayed almost the same. The people of Venezuela want to continue to enjoy the river's beauty and animals.

There are now several national parks and rain forest **preserves**[14] in the delta. These parks and preserves will help this great river remain an important natural resource for Venezuela. For now, the great Orinoco River is safe. It can continue to support the birds, animals, and people that depend on it.

---

[14] **preserve:** an area of land used to protect wild plants and animals

After You Read

1. The Orinoco River flows _____ the mountains _____ the sea.
   A. under, into
   B. down, from
   C. from, to
   D. to, and

2. A good heading for page 8 is:
   A. Water Is Area for Travel Only
   B. Orinoco Used for Hundreds of Years
   C. Orinoco Only Helps Yanomami Culture
   D. River Is Important to Local Cultures

3. What does the writer think about the rain forest?
   A. It's always dangerous.
   B. It's varied and interesting.
   C. It's safe to swim there.
   D. It's a quiet place.

4. Why is the jaguar special?
   A. It is the biggest rodent.
   B. It is the longest animal.
   C. It is a large type of snake.
   D. none of the above

5. In paragraph 2, on page 12, 'it' refers to the:
   A. crocodile
   B. capybara
   C. anaconda
   D. jaguar

6. On page 15, the phrase 'have grown significantly' can be replaced by:
   A. have grown a lot
   B. have not really grown
   C. have reduced in size
   D. have stayed the same

7. In the last fifty years, _____ cities and towns have gotten bigger.
   A. some
   B. all
   C. no
   D. almost all

8. The cities and towns along the delta show that the area is:
   A. totally natural
   B. changing
   C. staying the same
   D. very quiet

9. Which is NOT a sign of industry?
   A. river water
   B. electricity
   C. companies
   D. big ships

10. Why are rain forest preserves necessary in the Orinoco area?
   A. to allow people to build more
   B. to develop towns
   C. to protect the natural areas
   D. to help the companies

11. The Orinoco must continue to _____ people and animals near it.
   A. enjoy
   B. help
   C. depend on
   D. support

'Exploring Our World'

an interview with Dr. Bernard Thompson

Judy: Hello. This is Judy Jamison here with our weekly science program, 'Exploring Our World.' Here to talk with us this week is the well-known scientist, Dr. Bernard Thompson. In 2007, Dr. Thompson spent a year in the Amazon Rain Forest studying the local plant and animal life. Welcome, Dr. Thompson!

Dr. Thompson: Thank you, Judy. I'm happy to be here.

Judy: So, can you tell us a little about your work?

Dr. Thompson: Certainly! I'm interested in helping protect all forms of life in the forest. This includes everything from the beautiful jaguars on the land, to the piranhas in the rivers. We also want to protect their environment as well. We want to save the trees that make up the rain forest and keep the rivers clean.

Judy: And what did you learn on your latest trip?

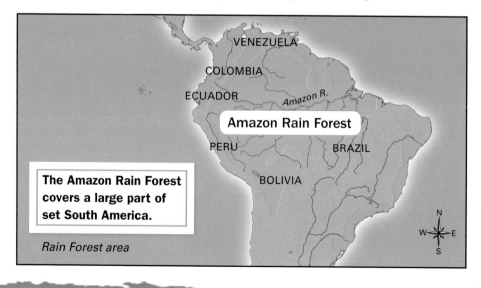

The Amazon Rain Forest covers a large part of set South America.

Rain Forest area

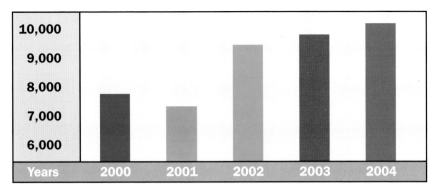

Square Miles of Rain Forest Lost Each Year

Dr. Thompson:	Unfortunately, I learned some things that really worried me. Did you know the rain forest is becoming smaller and smaller every year? Data shows that in the year 2000, the area lost about 7,500 square miles of forest. In 2004, we lost over 10,000 square miles!
Judy:	What are the causes of this?
Dr. Thompson:	Some large companies are cutting down a lot of the trees. They want to get to the natural resources in the area. Some are looking for oil. Others are looking for gold and diamonds. Farmers are also clearing a lot of the land. Wood from the trees has also become a valuable product all over the world. It's a big problem!
Judy:	Yes, it sounds serious.
Dr. Thompson:	It is. And in order to help people get these valuable resources, some governments are building roads. These roads are bringing more people and machines to the area. This means that the rain forest will continue to be cut down quickly.
Judy:	What will happen if the current situation doesn't change?
Dr. Thompson:	Well, according to recent theories, the rain forest could be gone within 30 years. . .

CD 1, Track 10

Word Count: 324
Time: _____

Vocabulary List

anaconda (3, 12, 13)

ancient (4)

capybara (3, 12, 13)

crocodile (3, 12, 13)

dam (16)

delta (2, 4, 7, 8, 15, 18)

diamond (16, 17)

flow (4, 7, 8)

gold (16, 17)

jaguar (3, 12, 13, 14)

mountain (2, 4)

natural resource (8, 18)

ocean (2, 4, 7, 16)

oil (16, 17)

paddle (8, 9)

piranha (3, 11)

plains (2, 4, 12, 13)

preserve (18)

rain forest (2, 4, 11, 12, 13, 18)

river (2, 4, 7, 8, 11, 12, 13, 15, 16, 18)

rodent (12)

stream (2, 7)

waterfall (2, 4, 7)